LOVE
your Beautiful

LOVE
your Beautiful

YOLANDA LEWIS

Extreme Overflow Publishing
A division of Extreme Overflow Enterprises, Inc
Grayson, Georgia 30017
www.extremeoverflow.com

Copyright ©2016
Published by Extreme Overflow Publishing
Photography Credit: Kim's Photography
www.kttphotography.com

Unless otherwise noted, all Scripture quotations are taken from the Life Application Study Bible, New International Version.

Manufactured in the United States of America
10 9 8 7 6 5 4 3 2 1

ISBN: 978-0-9976256-9-1

TABLE OF CONTENTS

INTRODUCTION

ABOUT THE AUTHOR

INTRODUCTION

You are enough no matter what anyone else thinks of you.

You are loveable and deserving of the utmost respect.

You are valuable to the world around you.

You are strong and have survived much.

You are bold and courageous inspiring others to dream.

You are beautiful, fearfully and wonderfully created to enjoy the uniqueness that makes you

REMARKABLE!

DID YOU KNOW...

that there are billions of people on this planet, but only one you? You have an original fingerprint, hair follicle and dental cavity that identifies you; different from everyone else. Meaning you are intentionally amazing and unique by design.

There is beauty in uniqueness. Loving that beauty is not a selfish or vain concept, unless you only see beauty from an external perspective. Owning your beauty and loving yourself has very little to do with outer appearances, exclusively. Beauty, real beauty, starts from within by having a healthy appreciation for your inner self. This inner beauty is what makes the light of your soul shine as a reflection of God's power, grace and omnipotence. It also helps others find their way out of the darkness of low self worth; your beauty has a purpose far beyond exhibition.

Having a healthy appreciation for how you were created honors the Creator. He would not have emphasized through scripture, that you are fearfully and wonderfully made, if He didn't find it important for you to remember that along your journey.

The way you were raised, may have convinced you otherwise. Social media images of filtered faces and altered bodies may have intimated you. Maybe a bad relationship has convinced you that your beauty is unworthy of acknowledgment. Perhaps you were abused or taken advantage of and those experiences have convinced you to hide what you were once sure was indeed beauty. Well guess what? You're not alone. In today's society, true beauty has been filtered, covered up and removed right from under our eyes. As a culture the imitation of beauty is celebrated in art, literature, film and music. The end result leaves young and seasoned women miserable, committing suicide, wanting to look like someone else, unhappy in their relationships and secretly lacking confidence through displays of superficiality; masked as self-assurance. A growing number of women feel un-beautiful when standing against the standard of what others define as beauty.

For every positive situation there is a negative one to take away from the positive moment. Negative situations, whether you have control over them or not come to steer your mind, heart, soul and body away from its purpose. The goal of negativity is to get you to overlook, ignore and squash the beauty of YOU; no matter who initiates that negative influence. Sure there are some things you can't stop from happening. However you can choose not to believe the negative remnants that are left after those events have long ended.

When you live beyond an experience; you live to tell the story of what you went through. At that point you have the choice to live in a beautiful place. For in that moment you have the option to rid yourself of the poisoned ideas that say you're not worth it, or you'll never be the best or even feeling like you aren't good enough. Your very presence confirms that there is something inside of you that is greater than any obstacle that may arise and try to stop you. The challenge comes in believing it.

Letting go of negative ideals that have been embedded in your mind for years or even generations is a process. You may not have realized it but over time you formed a habit in embracing these negative mind filters that break down everything positive you try to accomplish personally; in business or career and in relationships. You almost can't help being negative when it is a habit. But there is hope. Any habit can be broken in 21 days.

This book guides you in breaking the bad habit of not loving the true essence of you. Only you; your honesty, dedication, commitment, tenacity, and fight, can breakthrough to the beautiful life God designed for you to live.

Throughout your 21 day journey, you may

find that the process hurts and you need more paper to write! Take your time. Give it your all. Sacrifice. Fight for the revelation at the end. It may be very tempting to return to what you're used to, but it will be worth it to continue through the process to the end. You are worth it. You are beautiful. Love it!

QUESTION OF THE DAY:
WHAT WAS I THINKING?

....

Love your beautiful...
MIND!

Loving your beautiful mind is all about loving the decision to choose you first. You will be no good to everyone else if you are not first good to yourself.

Loving your beautiful mind also represents making the decision to be ok with and let go of your past.

1

There is a difference between forgetting past hurts and actually healing from them. When something is healed, there is no point of entry. There is no way to open the pain back up and hurt again. While there may be a scar, there is no wound.

It is possible to forgive and even forget what someone did to you, said to you or even how they made you feel. But you are forever engraved with what you chose to believe about yourself and about who you are after those experiences have occurred. Who you believe yourself to be after those painful experiences shape the attitudes you put out to the world today. Here you thought you were just pms'ing. Nope, the warring you are

2

experiencing comes from the conflict between what you have believed yourself to be and what you were created to be. Your constant fight with your mind is because God wants to enlighten you with his design. His design is first to know that no matter what man or woman his violated you, offended you, or no matter how un-pretty or how fat or too skinny they made you feel, you must know that He created you with beauty in mind. You are beautiful.

Wishing for the familiar and uncomfortable days of yesterday does nothing for today's discomfort. Today's discomfort will never go away if you are stuck in the past. To move forward and further away from the old you is a power God has given you through choice. Your mind controls all of that. Your mind is what makes today matter and tomorrow great. Understanding and embracing this empowers you to love what makes you beautiful. Stop taking on other people's problems. Stop believing what they spoke out of hurt. Decide to redefine and psyche your mind into believing that your journey; mistakes and all, do not make you un-beautiful. Remind yourself that your decision to move forward resonates exactly what makes you beautiful.

QUESTION OF THE DAY:
WHAT DO YOU LOVE ABOUT YOUR BODY?

· ·

Love your beautiful...
BODY!

"I wish I had a bigger butt, bigger breast, whiter teeth, smaller waist, thinner thighs," women say all the time. The question is why? What's wrong with what you've got? Who told you it wasn't enough? How many women do you know that wish they could change at least one thing about their body?

5

Through breast implants, butt shots, Jell-O shots…well maybe not Jell-O shots, but women are injecting their bodies with all types of "stuff" and in all types of ways for many different reasons.

Enhancing your beauty and altering your appearance to look like someone else is two completely different things. Perhaps you are a lady who would like to make a few body enhancements. Do you! But consider heavily whether or not you can truly live with who you will see in the mirror afterward. If you can live with that woman, than go for it.

Other ways to enhance your body image can happen by changing your eating habits and

6

exercising.

When I was thin, I wanted to be thick. Now that I am thick, I'd prefer not to have the tummy. My problem is that I love food. I loved it when I was thin and I still love it as a thicker woman. The difference is what I chose to make a priority. When I was smaller, I didn't eat on a schedule. I ate when I wanted to. I ate what I wanted to and there wasn't a second thought to it.

Within my see saw of a weight loss journey I have made food a priority. I focused too heavily on what to eat, when to eat and how much to eat adding stress to my life; which is another cause of weight gain.

7

When I was thin and oh so fabulous, I didn't know it. I suffered from low self esteem that hid behind many secrets of sexual abuse. Nonetheless, because I was thin, I didn't pay attention to what my eating patterns were or what my thoughts were about food. My focus was making sure my secrets never got out, in fear of getting in trouble; which was a trick the devil deceived me into believing. Sexual abuse as a child (I was 3 at my first encounter) is never your fault. However, I believed the lie and spent many years holding a secret that God would later set me free from. You can read my first book, "The Power of Deliverance," for more on that part of my life.

Once I became free, I just wanted to be happy; no more secrets, no more hiding, no more torment, just free to be myself. By the time I arrived at this place of freedom, I was married with children and dealing with another problem.

My freed soul felt trapped in a thick body that I did not have a clue how to "work." I was conflicted because everything about this thicker world seemed foreign. I didn't look how I used to; my waist was fuller, breast had tripled in size, and legs and thighs had thickened. I went from a size 6 to a size 12 (where I am now) and it was just a lot to embrace; although I was happy to finally have some cleavage in my shirts.

I found myself struggling in trying to figure out how this peaceful soul could appreciate the full figured shell I was now living in. I felt in between; not fat or skinny. It was an awkward moment inside and out. So, more soul searching commenced and the deeper I went within the more I wanted to cover up my appearance.

I went through a frumpy, hand me down only, never shop for myself, period. I was emotionally overwhelmed with so much change going on within me at once.

Change is easy, said no one ever. But what I learned was that change will get you to a place of transition. And transition sets you

10

on the path of new beginnings and bright futures.

Eventually I grew to the place where I began to look in the mirror and see what God saw; His beautiful precious and not tainted, daughter. I was valuable and loved.

Today, I am happy with my size. I'm happy with what I see. Who knows, maybe one day I'll lose weight and get back down to a size 6 or 7. What I do know is I'm not going to put pressure on myself to get there.

Your size is not what makes your body beautiful. It's confidence in your body that exudes beauty. Confidence or Godfidence in the totality of you, is a characteristic that comes from above and no one can take from you.

Go ahead, lose weight, wear makeup, waist trainers and the like; work it! Just be careful to know that you are beautiful with or without the enhancements.

Love your
beautiful...
SOUL

Everyone says they want to be in a healthy relationship but not everyone wants to do the work. Of the few people that say they are willing to do the work, even less are willing to be accountable to their faults.

Relationship is a growing concept for

13

everyone engaged. Male or female, friendship or marriage, relationship is a challenge. The challenge is in the risk. How much of your pride, ego, education, relational bucketed categories and belief systems are you willing to risk, sacrifice, or compromise in order to share or keep peace in your relationship?

Let's make it real. While you may know better than to argue with a fool because someone from afar can't tell which one of you is the crazy one, depending on the cause many will risk it all; pride ego, education and belief systems, to make their point heard in the situation. Sound familiar?

Conflict in relationship requires the effort (the work) of all individuals having the same goaled outcome to resolve the intensity of their differences. How you handle conflict is a reflection of how you see yourself in the situation. How you see yourself in the situation is a reflection of your inner person.

Do you see the need to compete at who's meaner, stronger, wittier, etc... To be successful at life and loving the skin you're in, you must be able to deal with conflict. Dealing with conflict begins with being responsible for you. Being responsible for you commences from depths of your being. It's important to look at what is really coming out of you in that moment of conflict. What emotion is driven forward? That is the one that needs to be worked on.

You are the only one responsible for your response. You have no control over how the other person chooses to respond. Know the power of your choice and dig deep in doing the work.

QUESTION OF THE DAY:
I SEE THE VISION, WHY CAN'T I HAVE IT?

Love your beautiful....
PURPOSE!

Everyone has a purpose. However, there is no specific age or time in which your purpose is revealed. Purpose is not restricted by time or defined by an age. Yet when it is revealed, it will be undeniable. It will click within and be the one thing in life you can't

17

shake. It calls you, drives you and moves you closer to it. While it grows clearer along the way, your days living in the land of purpose will not be filled with only sunshine and gumdrops. When those rainy, soggy, gray days come, it doesn't mean you're off track or going the wrong way. It also doesn't mean that you won't make any mistakes along the way. In most cases it is a clear indication of you going in the right direction.

Do you feel disorganized and scatter brained? When you're a talented fearless woman, sometimes it's hard to figure out that one thing you're good at. The thought alone may even exhaust you. Often times the

18

way you find your purpose is inspired by some type of failure. The pain that any one of your failures may have caused is what brings passion to your purpose. Why? Because when you fell down, you got back up. When you were tired and the only one to feed your children's mouths, go to school and try to be an example they could model after, you stood up, and showed up. When you couldn't see your way and cried too many tears to count, you looked up. That is what helps people, the fact that you made it. That is what defines purpose. In all of what you endured, there was one constant; one thing that never changed and this is where your true purpose can be found. Don't stop searching for it.

Love your beautiful...
YOU!

How bad do you want a better life for yourself? How bad do you want to experience a greater sense of purpose and feel complete where you belong? There are more women who are unhappy with themselves than not. Statistics show that 56% of women hate their bodies, 82% of marriages end in divorce, 62% of women have no idea what to do with their lives and young women are following suit. The list of unhappiness can go on for days.

It's time for each and every person to begin looking at their life from a different angle; a happy angle, a stress-less angle, a peaceful angle, a centered angle, a thankful angle. You get it, right? Make everyday a day that you love yourself, love what makes you beautiful and appreciate your life while focusing on the things you DO have and CAN attain. For this is when you will find love; loving your beautiful!

• •

Love your beautiful...
JOURNEY!

In the next 21 days you will dig deep to identify what makes your beautiful, connect with the inner beauty God placed inside of you, learn to embrace the skin you're in, and love your life on a new level. It is never too late to start loving your beauty. Go for it!

LOVING YOUR *Beautiful* BODY

WEEK 1

PRAYER: Lord, show me your ways and teach me your truth. I know it is through you that I gain clear understanding and power to recognize the beauty you created in me. Give me the desire to love myself and the confidence to enjoy the peace that comes from living in total obedience to your commands. I stand in gratitude and awe of your power.

Your Daughter,
Me

Day 1

Create a list of all the things you love about yourself when you look in the mirror. Read it and add to it often.

_____

_____

_____

_____

_____

_____

_____

_____

Day 2

Become aware of what your body can do each day. Remember it is the instrument of your life, not just an ornament.

_____

_____

_____

_____

_____

_____

_____

Day 3

Consider this: Your skin replaces itself once a month, your stomach lining every five days, your liver every six weeks, and your skeleton every three months. Your body is extraordinary! What can you do today to respect and appreciate it?

_____

_____

_____

_____

_____

_____

_____

Day 4

It's ok. There are no mistakes. There is no pressure to rush your way through life, not even to work out. So from this moment forward when you wake up, thank your body for resting and rejuvenating itself so you can enjoy the day.

_____

_____

_____

_____

_____

_____

_____

Day 5

Starting today, every evening you go to bed, tell your body how much you appreciate what it has allowed you to do throughout the day.

_____

_____

_____

_____

_____

_____

_____

_____

33

Day 6

Find a method of exercise that you enjoy
and do it regularly. Don't exercise to lose
weight or to fight your body. Do it to make
yourself feel good from the inside out.

_____

_____

_____

_____

_____

_____

_____

_____

Day 7

Think back to a time in your life when you felt good about your body. Tell yourself you can feel like that again, even in the body you have at this age.

_____

_____

_____

_____

_____

_____

_____

_____

LOVING YOUR Beautiful MIND

WEEK 2

PRAYER: Lord, show me who I am in you. I know that I am not perfect. Help me to let go of my past completely. Let me see my worth through your eyes. Remind me of my unique nature and quiet the voices that contradict your truth. Give me ears to hear the sound of your voice and your voice alone so that I can make decisions that reflect the magnitude of beauty you have bestowed me. Help me to know my beauty is shining through you and not only through what is tangible. I stand in gratitude and awe of your power.

Your Daughter,
Me

Day 8

Mind reformation: Think about the
moments and experiences that have altered
how you view beauty. Write it/them down.

_____

_____

_____

_____

_____

_____

_____

Day 9

Mind reformation: Do you believe you are naturally beautiful? Why? Why not?
.

_____

_____

_____

_____

_____

_____

_____

_____

Day 10

Mind reformation: What does beautiful mean to you? Create your own definition of what beautiful is. Write it down.

_____

_____

_____

_____

_____

_____

_____

_____

Day 11

Mind reformation: For 1 week, put a sign on each of your mirrors saying, "I'm beautiful inside and out."

_____

_____

_____

_____

_____

_____

_____

_____

Day 12

Mind reformation: Write a letter to yourself about your experience with beauty. Go back to the place it was tarnished and help your old self recover. Be your friend and supporter, not an enemy.

_____

_____

_____

_____

_____

_____

_____

Day 13

Mind reformation: Look at the world around you. List all of the beautiful things you see.

_____

_____

_____

_____

_____

_____

_____

_____

_____

_____

Day 14

Mind reformation: Loving your beautiful mind is about being open to filling it with nurturing food. Write the ways you can continue to develop beautiful thought.

_____

_____

_____

_____

_____

_____

_____

_____

LOVING YOUR *Beautiful* SPIRIT

WEEK 3

PRAYER: Lord, pour your light into my soul and expose the missing pieces I cannot see. Fill and seal every opening with your love. If there is any emotional, chemical, psychological, physical or spiritual imbalance set it to work in divine order. Help me to avoid the people, places and things that will only harm my spirit and steer me away from the divine power you have given to me in taking care of my temple. I stand in gratitude and awe of your power.

Your Daughter,
Me

Day 15

There is no exterior beauty without interior
love. What can you do to cultivate pure love
in your life?

_____

_____

_____

_____

_____

_____

_____

_____

Day 16

Start saying to yourself, "Life is too short to waste my time hating anything about me. I am beautiful and I love it!"

_____

_____

_____

_____

_____

_____

_____

_____

Day 17

Surround yourself with people that remind
you of your inner strength and beauty.

_____

_____

_____

_____

_____

_____

_____

_____

_____

Day 18

Walk with your head up, supported by God and confidence in your highest self as a person. He created you wonderful, fearless, and beautiful beyond measure.

_____

_____

_____

_____

_____

_____

_____

_____

Day 19

In thinking of every moment you've
endured, what was the one thing that stayed
constant?

_____

_____

_____

_____

_____

_____

_____

_____

_____

What did you learn from that constant?

_____

_____

_____

_____

_____

_____

_____

_____

_____

_____

_____

_____

_____

_____

_____

_____

_____

_____

_____

_____

_____

How did you make your life better from

what you learned?

_____

_____

_____

_____

_____

_____

_____

_____

_____

_____

How can you make someone else's life

better from what you learned?

_____

_____

_____

_____

_____

_____

_____

_____

_____

_____

Day 20

Think about all of the things you could
accomplish with the time and energy you
currently spend worrying about your body
and appearance. Write them down. Try one!

_____

_____

_____

_____

_____

_____

_____

Day 21

Count your blessings, not your blemishes.

_____

_____

_____

_____

_____

_____

_____

_____

_____

IN CLOSING

DAY 22!

Celebrating your beauty gives your Creator glory. Not with vanity or empty superficial adorning of the outer shell, but celebrating through owning it, living it and being beautiful, without baggage, without doubt, without fear, but in freedom to love, live and enjoy your life, your look and hope for a bright future.

So, behold my sister-queen, God is doing a new thing in you. This is the year of the Lord's favor for your life. He has plans to prosper even your seed.

84

Get ready for the overflow when your beauty begins to shine; it will come quickly. Position yourself, your business and your mind to receive the unfathomable; a peace that surpasses all understanding.

As you glow in the light of God's beauteous favor, move forward in loving what makes you beautiful. Appreciate your journey for what it is. Remove selfishness, anxiety, and poor temperament. Break down the walls of old habits, emotional mindsets and self protecting behaviors. Soften your heart to see your beauty the way God sees it, overflowing in his love. With God's power you will do magnificent things. It will be beautiful, exactly the way God made you.

85

ABOUT THE
AUTHOR

• •

Y O L A N D A   L E W I S

As a business woman, mother, and wife I have firsthand experience with the difficulties of trying to figure out the balance of purpose, peace, and beauty in life.

I remember the first time I received a real job promotion. My good friend was proud of me and wanted to buy me my first power suit. We went to a large department store and she told me to pick out whatever suit I wanted.

I went through the clearance rack in search of my first real suit. My friend also browsed. As we searched, she asked me, "Do you see anything you like?" I said "Yes, I see a few things but they are out of my price range." She quickly responded, "Price rage? I told you this was my treat." Then she proceeded to show me different suits, "What about this one?' she said. I would look at the suit and then look at the price tag and put it back on the rack. Finally my friend asked me why I keep putting things back and I broke down crying.

The problem was that I had never spent more than twenty dollars on myself. When shopping for my children or even buying gifts for my husband I spent limitlessly. But for myself, I felt anything more than twenty dollars was just too much.

My friend consoled me and told me it was ok and that I didn't have to get a suit if I was that uncomfortable. She offered to buy my slacks instead. Eventually I declined and left the store with nothing. The experience was overwhelming but it brought me tremendous revelation as to where I put my value and my worth.

It wasn't until later in life that I embraced what God describes through the scriptures as being fearfully and wonderfully created by Him. It wasn't until later that I actually believed that and let it show in how I cared for my appearance. I learned that to not value God's creation is a complete insult to the beauty the creator has entrusted you with.

It is my hope that this book has inspired you to consider your value. Consider your Creator and the fact that He makes no mistakes in who is gifted with the breath of life here on earth. When you love what makes you beautiful you are just one step closer to living a beautiful life; one that will warm your spirit and make God smile.

Check out these other fascinating titles by:
YOLANDA LEWIS

Available for order at:

www.extremeoverflow.com

References

McMinn, M. R. (1996). *Psychology, theology, and spirituality in Christian counseling.* Carol Stream, IL: Tyndale House.

Berns, R. M. (2016). Child, family, school, community: Socialization and support. Boston, MA Cengage Learning

Moyer, M. S. (2005). *Investigating and understanding self-harming behaviors in adolescents: A phenomenological study.* (Order No. 3189185, Texas A&M University - Corpus Christi). *ProQuest Dissertations and Theses, ,* 157-157 p. Retrieved from http://search.proquest.com.library.capella.edu/docvie w/305378284?accountid=27965 (305378284)

Zayas, L.H. (2012). Are suicide attempts by Latinas a cultural idom of distress. Transcultural Psychiatry-Sage Journals (49)5, 718-734. Doi: 10.1177/1363461512463262

Warren, B. J., & Broome, B. (2011). The culture of mental illness in adolescents with urologic problems. *Urologic Nursing, 31*(2), 95-103,111. Retrieved from http://search.proquest.com.library.capella.edu/docvie w/861922814?accountid=27965

Made in the USA
Middletown, DE
22 May 2016